Castle Dracula

Romania's Vampire Home

By Barbara J. Knox

Consultant: Stephen F. Brown, Director
Institute of Medieval Philosophy and Theology, Boston College

BEARPORT
PUBLISHING COMPANY, INC.

New York, New York

Credits

Cover José Fuste Raga / CORBIS; title page, Jose Fuste Raga / CORBIS

Background portrait throughout, The Granger Collection, New York; 4-5, Romanian National Tourist Office; 5, Universal / The Kobal Collection; 8, 9, Photofest; 10, Dinu Lazar; 11, The Kobal Collection; 12, British Library Images Online; 13, The Granger Collection, New York; 14, The Pierpont Morgan Library / Art Resource, NY; 15, The Art Archive / British Library / British Library; 16, Dinu Lazar; 17 (left), Tom Kinter; 17 (right), MirrorImage; 18, Erich Lessing / Art Resource, NY; 19, The Granger Collection, New York; 20-21, Tom Kinter; 21, Romanian National Tourist Office; 22, 23, Tom Kinter; 24, Romanian National Tourist Office; 25, Eugene Schultz; 26, Romanian National Tourist Office; 26-27, Rodica Prato; 29, Jose Fuste Raga / CORBIS.

Design and production by Dawn Beard Creative, Triesta Hall of Blu-Design, and Octavo Design and Production, Inc.

Special thanks to the Romanian Cultural Center in New York City and the Romanian National Tourist Office in New York City.

Library of Congress Cataloging-in-Publication Data

Knox, Barbara.
  Castle Dracula : Romania's vampire home / by Barbara J. Knox ; consultant, Stephen Brown.
    p. cm. — (Castles, palaces & tombs)
  Includes bibliographical references and index.
  ISBN 1-59716-000-8 (lib. bdg.)—ISBN 1-59716-023-7 (pbk.)
  1. Castelul Bran (Bran, Brasov, Romania)—Juvenile literature. 2. Vlad III, Prince of Wallachia, 1430 or 31-1476 or 7—Juvenile literature. 3. Castles—Romania—Bran (Brasov)—Juvenile literature. 4. Romania—History—To 1711—Juvenile literature. 5. Dracula, Count (Fictitious character)—Juvenile literature. I. Brown, Stephen F. II. Title. III. Series.

  DR240.5.V553K59 2005
  949.8'4—dc22

                        2004020986

For more information, write to Bearport Publishing Company, Inc., 101 Fifth Avenue, Suite 6R, New York, New York 10003. Printed in the United States of America.

                        3 4 5 6 7 8 9 10

Table of Contents

A Vampire!

Under a bright moon, thick fog swirled around the dark castle. The building's high towers seemed to touch the night sky. Something evil lived inside.

Castle Dracula

Suddenly, a creature in a long, black cape crawled down the castle wall. He moved silently through the woods toward the village.

Moments later, he saw a house with an open window. Inside, a young woman slept. She slept, that is, until the fangs of a **vampire** pierced her neck!

In stories, vampires often take the shape of bats, wolves, snakes, and other animals.

Birth of a Vampire

In 1897, a writer named Bram Stoker wrote a book called *Dracula*. Stoker's book is based on **legends** about people who drank blood. It's also based, however, on the life of a real prince named Vlad.

PACIFIC
OCEAN

NORTH
AMERICA

N
W E
S

SOUTH
AMERICA

Was Vlad really a vampire? No, but many people feared him. From 1456 to 1462, he ruled part of Romania, a country in eastern Europe. Vlad protected his people, but he was cruel to his enemies. He **impaled** them by sticking sharp poles through their bodies. Vlad's **victims** all died horrible deaths.

Vlad's father was called Dracul, which means "dragon." Dracula was Vlad's nickname. It means "son of the dragon."

Dracula, the Movie

Years after Stoker wrote his book, movies were made about the story. The most famous one came out in 1931. It is also called *Dracula*.

A scene from the movie *Dracula*

Thousands of people stood in line to see the movie. They screamed when Dracula rose from his **coffin**. They gasped when his dark home, Castle Dracula, was shown on screen. Some people even ran from the theater when they saw the vampire's bloody fangs.

Many people loved the story, though. They wanted to know more about vampires. They also wondered if there really was such a castle.

The first movie based on the Dracula story came out in 1922. It was called *Nosferatu*.

The Real Castle Dracula

In 1377, a king rebuilt a castle that sat high up on a rocky hill in a village called Brasov. He wanted a place where soldiers could watch over their city and protect it.

Bran Castle

The building was named Bran Castle. It was in a part of Romania called Transylvania. Hundreds of years ago, people there believed vampires were real. Villagers stayed out of the woods after dark. They locked their doors every night.

When the Dracula movie came out, people were told that Stoker based his story on Vlad. They also found out that Vlad once lived in Bran Castle.

A scene from the movie *Dracula*

Bran Castle came to be called Castle Dracula after the 1931 movie *Dracula.*

Life in the Middle Ages

Bran Castle was built in a time called the **Middle Ages**. Fighting was a part of everyday life. Kings killed for power. **Lords** fought over land. Huge armies marched to far-off places to fight about religion.

Enemies often used ladders to get over castle walls.

In Vlad's day, a soldier always stood guard in the castle's lookout tower. If he spotted an enemy, he yelled for the people of the town to run to the castle for safety. Then guards shut the heavy wooden door. **Archers** raced up to the towers. Their arrows flew through **fire holes**. Soldiers threw rocks down on the enemy. Screams filled the air.

Castle soldiers tried their best to push the ladders away.

In the Middle Ages, most people died before they were 35 years old.

Building Bran Castle

The original Bran Castle had been a **fortress**. Turkish soldiers burned it to the ground in 1370. While the castle was being rebuilt, most of the village's men, women, and children worked on it. They made the new castle much stronger than the old one.

In the Middle Ages, almost all work, such as cooking, was done by hand.

Men cut huge stone blocks near the river. Horses dragged the blocks to where the castle was being built. There, **masons** made cement from sand, water, and lime to hold the stones in place.

The women baked bread and cooked wild birds for food. Children carried water from the river in wooden buckets.

After villagers worked all day on the castle, they had chores to do at home.

Children in the Middle Ages often went to work when they turned seven years old.

Towers, Secret Rooms, and Murder Holes!

At last, Bran Castle was finished. Its white stone walls sparkled in the sunlight. From far away, the red roofs of its towers looked like pointed hats.

Inside, the new castle held many surprises. Hidden stairways led to secret rooms. A maze of passages was built under the courtyard. Hidden tunnels led out to the valley.

Murder holes were added to one tower in the 1400s. Castle soldiers poured boiling water on the enemy through these holes. The people screamed as the water hit them. They died slow, painful deaths from the burns.

A secret stairway in Bran Castle

An example of a fire hole from Warkworth Castle in England

Soldiers in the Middle Ages used crossbows. These powerful weapons could shoot arrows through metal armor.

Vlad the Impaler

In 1456, Prince Vlad came to power. His army fought fierce battles against the Turks.

Vlad hated the Turks. Once, he impaled hundreds of Turkish soldiers. Then he sat down near their bodies and ate dinner.

Prince Vlad

Vlad killed women and children. He also chopped off the heads of lords. In 1459, he ordered 20,000 Turks impaled. The bodies hung on the **stakes** for weeks.

Turkish soldiers killed Vlad in 1476. When his body was found, his head was gone. What happened to it? To this day, no one knows.

Prince Vlad, surrounded by people he has impaled, enjoys a meal.

Visitors once forgot to take off their hats in front of Vlad. The angry prince nailed their hats to their heads!

Peace at Last

Long after Vlad's death, peace finally came to Transylvania. By the 1600s, the soldiers were gone and the castle was a **trading post**. Grain and wood was stored in its rooms. Traders from India and China stopped by on their way to Europe. They bought cheese, milk, and meat.

The courtyard at the castle, where cheese, milk, and meat were sold

Still, the villagers wanted a strong castle. In 1622, they added another tower. More stone was added to the castle's back wall. When it was finished, the wall was 11 feet thick!

An overhead view of Bran Castle

Many castles had towers where soldiers went to keep watch.

A Royal Palace

By the 1900s, the castle's dark history seemed over. The weapons room sat empty. Prisoners no longer cried out from the basement.

In 1920, the people of Brasov gave Bran Castle to Romania's royal family. Queen Marie added expensive furniture and thick rugs. She turned the fire holes into windows.

Queen Marie at Bran Castle

Workers put an elevator in the courtyard. This way, the King and Queen could easily reach the underground passages. The royal children often rode the elevator. Then they skipped through the tunnels that led to the **valley**.

Queen Marie (in the middle) with her family

Visitors to the castle can see Queen Marie's 300-year-old bed.

The Modern Age

Romania has not had a king or queen since 1947. After the royal family left, Bran Castle sat empty for a few years. Then, in 1956, Romania gave the castle back to the people of Brasov. The people decided to use the castle as a museum. They filled it with furniture, weapons, and **armor** from all the people who ever lived there.

A part of Queen Marie's bedroom

Over the years, parts of the castle fell apart. In 1987, workers began to repair the building. After six years, the castle was finally **restored** to what it once was.

Another part of Queen Marie's bedroom

Glass windows were not widely used in castles until the 1700s.

Visiting Castle Dracula

Thousands of tourists visit Bran Castle every year. They begin the journey in Bucharest, Romania's capital. From there, they ride over narrow, winding roads into the mountains. Cows and pigs that wander into the road often slow the journey.

The castle sits on a 200-foot tall rock. It looks over the village of Bran.

Once at the castle, tourists are free to explore. They can peek down the tower's murder holes. They can climb up secret stairways. They can even imagine Vlad pacing the stone floors.

Bram Stoker's vampire story made the castle famous. It also turned Vlad into a legend!

North View

There was a secret staircase between the third and fourth floors.

The Gunpowder Tower had murder holes.

The dungeons were on the ground floor and the first floor.

South View

White stone walls

Red roofs cap the towers.

Bran Castle sits high up on a hill.

Just the Facts

❧ **Vampire Legends**

Vampires can be killed with a silver bullet.

Vampires do not like mirrors or silver crosses.

Vampires can climb the outside of castle walls.

❧ **Vlad the Impaler**

Vlad once invited poor and blind people to eat with him. When the meal was over, he locked them in the dining hall. Then he burned the hall to the ground.

Vlad learned about impaling from the Turks. In the Middle Ages, soldiers from many countries impaled enemies on stakes.

Some people who study history don't believe that Vlad lived for very long at Bran Castle. It's fairly certain, however, that he spent time there.

❧ **Brasov, Romania**

Brasov is the second largest city in Romania.

Some buildings in Brasov date back to the 1200s.

The people of Brasov started building a wall around the city in the 1300s. They finished it 400 years later.

Timeline

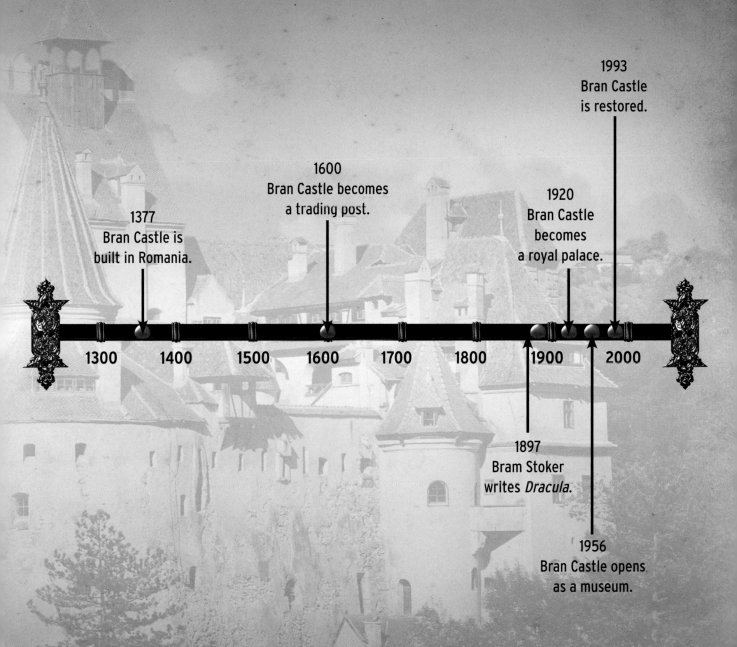

1993
Bran Castle
is restored.

1600
Bran Castle becomes
a trading post.

1920
Bran Castle
becomes
a royal palace.

1377
Bran Castle is
built in Romania.

1300 1400 1500 1600 1700 1800 1900 2000

1897
Bram Stoker
writes *Dracula*.

1956
Bran Castle opens
as a museum.

Glossary

archers (AR-churz) people who shoot at targets using a bow and arrow

armor (AR-mur) a suit made of metal worn to protect the body

coffin (KAWF-in) a long box in which a dead person is buried

fire holes (FIRE holz) narrow slit windows in castle walls used to shoot arrows through

fortress (FOR-triss) a large building or area that is strengthened against attacks

impaled (im-PAYLD) killed by piercing with a sharp stake

legends (LEJ-uhndz) stories handed down from long ago that are often based on some facts but cannot be proven true

lords (LORDZ) men who lived in castles and had great power during the Middle Ages (between the years 500 and 1450)

masons (MAY-suhnz) people whose work is building with stone, brick, or cement

Middle Ages (MID-uhl AJE-iz) the period of history in Europe from about the years 500 to 1450

restored (ri-STORD) returned to its original condition

stakes (STAYKS) sharp, pointed pieces of wood or metal that can be driven into the ground

trading post (TRADE-ing POHST) a store where people can trade local products for food and supplies

valley (VAL-ee) an area of low land between two mountains or hills, often with a river running through it

vampire (VAM-pire) in stories, a dead creature who rises from the grave to suck on the blood of people

victims (VIK-tuhmz) people who are hurt, injured, or killed by a person or event

Bibliography

Corbishley, Mike. *The Medieval World.* New York, NY: Peter Bedrick (1992).

Jordan, William Chester. *The Middle Ages: A Watts Guide for Children.* New York, NY: Franklin Watts (1999).

Kaufman, Deborah, and Douglas Stallings. *Fodor's Travel Guide to Eastern and Central Europe.* New York, NY: Random House (2001).

Klepper, Nicolae. *Romania: An Illustrated History.* New York, NY: Hippocrene Books, Inc. (2002).

McNeill, Sarah. *The Middle Ages.* New York, NY: Oxford University Press (1998).

Read More

Hutchinson, Emily. *Dracula* (Abridged Edition). Minneapolis, MN: Sagebrush Education Resources (1998).

Kudalis, Eric. *Dracula and Other Vampire Stories.* Mankato, MN: Capstone Press (1994).

Streissguth, Thomas. *Legends of Dracula.* Minneapolis, MN: Lerner Publications (1999).

Learn More Online

Visit these Web sites to learn more about Castle Dracula and Bran Castle:

http://www.brasovtravelguide.ro/bv-en/surroundings/dracula-castle.php

http://www.trueromanian.com/draculaMain.php

Index

About the Author

Barbara Knox saw the movie *Dracula* when she was a girl. She read Bram Stoker's *Dracula* when she was older. She likes vampire stories. Now her daughter, Annie, is curious about vampires, too. They would like to go "vampire camping" in Romania. Go to your library to find out more about vampire camping!